Quotable New York

Quotable New York

Compiled by
Gregg Stebben

THE LYONS PRESS
GUILFORD, CONNECTICUT
AN IMPRINT OF THE GLOBE PEQUOT PRESS

10 9 8 7 6 5 4 3 2 1

Printed in the United States of America

Library of Congress Cataloging-in-Publication Data is available on file.

ISBN 1-58574-569-3

In memory of those who died on September 11,
In honor of those who served in the aftermath.

Contents

Preface

What is a New Yorker? Think about it for even a moment and you'll realize the answer is a moving target.

My own experience mirrors that. Though I've lived in Manhattan for many years and consider myself thoroughly and irrevocably a New Yorker, I'm a native Californian, and other New Yorkers are quick to see the West Coast in me. Yet when I am on the West Coast, I am often mistaken for a New Yorker. Go figure. Could it be that I am both?

Compiling a book of quotes from New Yorkers requires one to know a New Yorker when he sees one. Now there's a stumper.

Is a New Yorker someone who was born in New York and has lived here all his or her life? Someone who was born in New York, but has since moved on? Someone who works in New York, but lives elsewhere? Visits frequently? Wishes he or she could visit frequently? Someone who subscribes to *The New York Times* and reads it every day or who pores over *The New Yorker* every week, albeit from many miles away? Could you be a New Yorker even if the closest you've ever come to the city is in your dreams?

Following the attacks on the World Trade Center in September 2001, people from all around the world raised the rallying cry that "We're all New Yorkers now!" Yet it didn't take tragedy to turn the world into a population of New Yorkers. The world has always followed New York's events, read its daily paper, *The New York Times*, watched its plays, and sung its tunes as if doing so were a way to participate and follow the daily events of America's national hometown. Meanwhile, some people just are "New York": Woody Allen, because he's, well, a little nuts. Robert DeNiro, because he's tough. Jacqueline Onassis, because she's glamorous. Frank Sinatra, because he was so, Frank Sinatra. Barbra Streisand, because she's set a stunning example of what a poor girl from Brooklyn can do when she sets her mind to it. Howard Stern, because he's always walking on the edge. Tom Wolfe, because he sees the world crisply and writes about it like nobody's business. Speaking of business, there's that New Yorker who's famous for the art of the deal, Donald Trump. And finally, let's not forget all those New Yorkers who are New Yorkers simply because they are funny and fascinating and alive and easy to love; Jerry Seinfeld, Fran Lebowitz, Billy Crystal, and Yogi Berra instantly come to mind.

If you want to play the "Who's a New Yorker?" game at home, debate this one among yourselves: Hillary Rodham Clinton. New Yorker?

She was born in Chicago. Lived in Arkansas most of her adult life. *Now*, bags packed quickly at her former home in the White House, she lives in New York for the first time, in the New York City suburb of Chappaqua.

Tough call, huh?

As you can begin to see, there are *several* underlying factors in the very name of this book, *Quotable New York*. First, as we've already discussed, there's the question, "What makes a New Yorker?" Second, *who better* to quote? After all, when you think of a group of people who love to talk and always have an opinion, the first group you think of is New Yorkers, right? Finally, there's an element of the absurd in the undertaking. While there are scores of thousands of quotable New Yorkers to choose from who are always ready and willing to tell you what they think, how could one ever decide *who* among the many to quote, sacrificing the wit and wisdom and humor and style of so many others?

Let me assure you, choosing which subjects and quotes to include was no easy task. I often made the final cuts with friends at my local pub over a cold Rolling Rock, or at my local coffee house over a double espresso. Occasionally the discussion would become so heated a good old-fashioned New York barroom brawl would threaten to erupt. But in the end, the job got done.

I hope you enjoy dipping into these quotations as much as I enjoyed collecting them.

Now if you'll excuse me, I've got to get back down to the street to see what I've been missing...

Why We Love New York

New York is to the nation what the white church spire is to the village—the visible symbol of aspiration and faith, the white plume saying the way is up.

E. B. WHITE, *MENTAL HEALTH IN THE METROPOLIS*

New York is the place where all the aspirations of the Western World meet to form one vast master aspiration, as powerful as the suction of a steam dredge. It is the icing on the pie called Christian civilization.

H. L. MENCKEN, *PREJUDICES*, SIXTH SERIES, 1927

The whole world revolves around New York. Very little happens anywhere unless someone in New York presses the button.

DUKE ELLINGTON

When Wall Street sneezes, the rest of the world catches a cold.

ANONYMOUS

I'd rather be a lamppost in New York than the mayor of Chicago.

JIMMY WALKER, MAYOR, 1926–1932

Something's always happening here. If you're bored in New York, it's your own fault.

MYRNA LOY

New York attracts the most talented people in the world in the arts and professions. It also attracts them in other fields. Even the bums are talented.

EDMUND LOVE, *SUBWAYS ARE FOR SLEEPING*

He speaks English with the flawless imperfection of a New Yorker.

GILBERT MILLSTEIN

Everyone in New York knows that he is an important person living among other important persons.

BRENDAN BEHAN, "WHERE WE ALL CAME INTO TOWN,"
EVERGREEN REVIEW

There are only about 400 people in fashionable New York society. If you go outside the number, you strike people who are either not at ease in a ballroom, or make other people not at ease. See the point?

WARD MCCALLISTER

One belongs to New York instantly. One belongs to it as much in five minutes as in five years.

THOMAS WOLFE, *THE WEB AND THE ROCK*, 1939

Manhattan is a machine, fueled by the millions of people who pour through its streets and subways each day, many of them locked in an exhausting but addictive life style which makes anywhere else seem dull and slow.

FIONA DUNCAN AND LEONIE GLASS

Other cities consume culture, New York creates it.

PAUL GOLDBERGER, *THE CITY OBSERVED*

———•••———

New York is where the future comes to audition.

ED KOCH, MAYOR, 1978–1989

New York, the nation's thyroid.

CHRISTOPHER MORLEY, *SHORE LEAVE*

The capital city of high-tension activity.

STANLEY LEVEY

New York has a trip-hammer vitality which drives you insane with restlessness, if you have no inner stabiliser.

HENRY MILLER, *THE COLUSSUS OF MAROUSSI*, 1941

The great days in New York were just before you got there.

LEWIS GANNETT, *COUNTRY JOURNAL*

She dreamed, lulled by the train, of getting off at heaven or New York City, whichever she got to first.

MARY LEE SETTLE

To step from a train platform into Grand Central's extraordinary concourse . . . is to feel in every fiber that you have arrived someplace important, to know that you have come into a great city and that great city has greeted you properly.

PAUL GOLDBERGER

New York is one of the finest cities I ever saw. . . . Situated on an island, which I think it will one day cover, it rises, like Venice from the sea, and receives into its lap tribute of all the riches of the earth.

FRANCES TROLLOPE, *DOMESTIC MANNERS OF THE AMERICANS*

What else can you expect from a town that's shut off from the world by the ocean on one side and New Jersey on the other?

O. HENRY, *A TEMPERED WIND, THE GENTLE GRAFTER*

A little strip of an island with a row of well-fed folks up and down the middle, and a lot of hungry folks on each side.

HARRY LEON WILSON, *THE SPENDERS*, 1902

The only credential the city asked was the boldness to dream. For those who did, it unlocked its gates and its treasures, not caring who they were or where they came from.

MOSS HART, *ACT ONE*, 1959

Here I was in New York, city of prose and fantasy, of capitalist automation, its streets a triumph of cubism, its moral philosophy that of the dollar. New York impressed me tremendously because, more than any other city in the world, it is the fullest expression of our modern age.

LEON TROTSKY, *MY LIFE*, 1930

Little has changed in our New York neighborhoods except the faces, the names, and the languages spoken. The same decent values of hard work and accomplishment and service to city and nation still exist.

DAVID DINKINS, MAYOR, 1990–1993

I think that New York is not the cultural center of America, but the business and administrative center of American culture.

SAUL BELLOW, IN A RADIO INTERVIEW, 1969

Every great wave of popular passion that rolls up on the prairies is dashed to spray when it strikes the hard rocks of Manhattan.

H. L. MENCKEN, *PREJUDICES*, FOURTH SERIES, 1925

The present in New York is so powerful that the past
is lost.

JOHN JAY CHAPMAN, LETTER, MARCH 26, 1898

The alive, pulsing city is the greatest artistic achieve-
ment of humankind.

DR. JAMES HILLMAN

New York has a life of its own, its own pulse, which beats just a bit faster than that of its inhabitants.

URI SAVIR, ISRAELI CONSUL GENERAL

———

New York is like disco, but without the music.

ELAINE STRITCH, *QUOTED OBSERVER*

New York's a small place when it comes to the part
of it that wakes up just as the rest is going to bed.

P. G. WODEHOUSE, *THE AUNT AND THE SLUGGARD*

Crazed with avarice, lust and rum,
New York, thy name's Delirium.

B. R. NEWTON, *OWED TO NEW YORK*

New York was no mere city. It was instead an infinitely romantic notion, the mysterious nexus of all love and money and power, the shining and perishable dream itself. To think of "living" there was to reduce the miraculous to the mundane; one does not "live" at Xanadu.

JOAN DIDION, *SLOUCHING TOWARD BETHLEHEM*

The beautiful city, the city of hurried and sparkling waters! The city of spires and masts!
The City nested in bays! My city!
The city of such women, I as mad with them! I will return after death to be with them!
The city of such young men, I swear I cannot live happy without I often go talk, walk, eat, drink, sleep with them!

WALT WHITMAN, *LEAVES OF GRASS*, 1900

I miss the animal buoyancy of New York, the animal vitality. I did not mind that it had no meaning and no depth.

ANAÏS NIN, *DIARIES*, VOL. 2

———

There is a great tango of eye contact between men and women on the streets of New York.

JOSEPH GIOVANNI

The great big city's a wondrous toy
Just made for a girl and boy
We'll turn Manhattan
Into an isle of joy.

LORENZO HART, *MANHATTAN*, 1925

———

This is the province of let's pretend located in the state of anomie.

GAIL SHEEHY, *HUSTLING*

New York, thy name is irreverence and hyperbole. And grandeur.

ADA LOUISE HUXTABLE, *NEW YORK TIMES* ARCHITECTURE CRITIC

The pavements of New York are filled with people escaping the prison sentence of personal history into the promise of an open destiny.

VIVIAN GORNICK, *THE NEW YORKER*

The lusts of the flesh can be gratified anywhere; it is not this sort of license that distinguishes New York. It is, rather, a lust of the total ego for recognition, even for eminence. More than elsewhere, everybody here wants to be somebody.

SYDNEY J. HARRIS

There are two million interesting people in New York—and only 78 in Los Angeles.

NEIL SIMON

Robinson Crusoe, the self-sufficient man, could not have lived in New York City.

WALTER LIPPMAN

Ah! Some love Paris,
And some love Perdue.
But love is an archer with a low I.Q.
A bold, bad bowman, and innocent of pity.
So I'm in love with
New York City.

PHYLLIS MCGINLEY

If Paris is the setting for a romance, New York is the perfect city in which to get over one, to get over anything. Here the lost *douceur de vivre* is forgotten and the intoxication of living takes over.

CYRIL CONNOLLY

I spend my summers in Europe and when they ask me if I'm an American, I say, "No, I'm a New Yorker."

ALEXANDER ALLAND, JR.

It's not so much that I'm an American. I'm a New Yorker.

NETHERLANDS-BORN WILLIAM DE KOONING

———

When it's three o'clock in New York, it's still 1938 in London.

ATTRIBUTED TO BETTE MIDLER

The networks don't recognize a story until it's in *The New York Times*.

JACK ANDERSON

When an American stays away from New York too long, something happens to him. Perhaps he becomes a little provincial, a little dead, a little afraid.

SHERWOOOD ANDERSON

Toronto is kind of New York operated by the Swiss.

JOHN BENTLY MAYS

New York is the meeting place of the peoples, the only city where you can hardly find a typical American.

DJUNA BARNES

New York is a different country. Maybe it ought to have a separate government. Everybody thinks differently, acts differently. They just don't know what the hell the rest of the United States is.

HENRY FORD

New York has total depth in every area. Washington has only politics; after that, the second biggest thing is white marble.

JOHN LINDSAY, MAYOR, 1966–1973

If 1,668,172 people are to be set down in one narrow strip of land between two quiet rivers, you can hardly improve on this solid mass of buildings and the teeming organism of human life that streams through them. For better or worse, this is real.

BROOKS ATKINSON

It's a city where everyone mutinies but no one deserts.

HARRY HERSHFIELD

What is barely hinted at in other American cities is condensed and enlarged in New York.

SAUL BELLOW

———

Personally, I've always favored New York 'cause this is one city where you don't have to ride in the back of the bus. Not that they're so liberal—it's just that in New York, nobody moves to the back of the bus.

DICK GREGORY, *FROM THE BACK OF THE BUS*

New York is the city of brotherly shove.

ANONYMOUS

———•—•—•———

Every person on the streets of New York is a type. The city is one big theater where everyone is on display.

JERRY RUBIN

I loved every single movie that was set in New York, every movie that began high above the New York skyline and moved in, every detective story, every romantic comedy, every movie about nightclubs in New York or penthouses.

WOODY ALLEN

For there is gaiety in this sprawling metropolis. You hear it in the cheep of sparrows in the park, the laughter of children in playgrounds. The banter of taxi drivers lightly insulting other motorists, and it is a truer gaiety than that which glitters in the night.

SISTER MARYANNA OF THE DOMINICAN ACADEMY

East side, west side, all around the town,
The tots sang ring-a-rosie, London Bridge is falling
 down;
Boys and girls together, me and Mamie O'Rourke,
Tripped the light fantastic on the sidewalks of New
 York

JAMES W. BLAKE

Manhattan crowds with their turbulent musical cho-
rus! Manhattan faces and eyes forever for me.

WALT WHITMAN, *LEAVES OF GRASS*, 1900

I would rather see the old reservoir on 42nd street or the original Madison Square Garden than I would any of the lost wonders of the ancient world.

LOUIS AUCHINCLOSS

If I live in New York, it is because I choose to live here. It is the city of total intensity, the city of the moment.

DIANE VREELAND

New York is an ugly city, a dirty city. Its climate is a scandal, its politics are used to frighten children, its traffic is madness, its competition is murderous. But once you have lived in New York and it has become your home no place else is good enough!

JOHN STEINBECK, "THE MAKING OF NEW YORK"

My favorite city in the world is New York. Sure it's dirty—but like a beautiful lady smoking a cigar.

JOAN RIVERS

Is "New York" the most beautiful city in the world? It is not far from it. No urban nights are like the nights there. I have looked down across the city from high windows. It is then that the great buildings lose reality and take on magical powers.

EZRA POUND

I've occasionally remarked that I can't imagine living anywhere other than New York, or doing anything other than writing. But how could that be true? Imagination is a writer's stock in trade.

LAWRENCE BLOCK

As soon as you feel you understand New York, an unpalatable fact becomes apparent: your understanding is obsolete.

JOHN GATTUSO

———•••———

Any attempt to define New York today recalls the Zen wisdom that you can't step in the same stream twice. The city is mutable, so constantly changing that it's almost impossible to get a fix on it. . . . Simply put, New York never gets boring. Anything can happen here.

CHERYL FARR LEAS

New York meets the most severe test that may be applied to the definition of a metropolis—it stays up all night. But also it becomes a small town when it rains.

JOHN GUNTHER

A haven as cosy as toast . . .

DYLAN THOMAS

New York will be a great place if they ever finish it.

O. HENRY

———•••———

There have been many days in New York when I was running for mayor, and then since I've been mayor, when I would have a weekend in which I would go to a mosque on Friday, a synagogue on Saturday, and a church—sometimes two churches—on a Sunday. And by the time I finished, I would say to myself, "I know that we're through to God." We're talking to him in every language that He understands.

RUDOLPH W. GIULIANI

Only in New York

If you ever had a desire to serve on a jury, I can assure you, professionally and personally, this will be a good one.

CHARLES SOLOMON, NEW YORK STATE SUPREME COURT JUSTICE, TO PROSPECTIVE JURORS FOR THE PUFF DADDY TRIAL

When he came into the great dining room at dinner time, and looked at all the tables thronged with members of the legislature and the lobby he never doubted that he could buy every man in the room if he were willing to pay the price.

GEORGE WILLIAM CURTIS, ON BOSS TWEED

One month after New York City began a test of six new sidewalk toilets, going to the bathroom has become New York's latest tourist attraction.

JONATHON RABINOWITZ, REPORTER, *THE NEW YORK TIMES*

We had one toilet for everyone on the floor. And I would sit for hours in the toilet and read Shakespeare. One girl would knock on the door and say, "Hey, Shakespeare, get out of there."

WALTER MATTHAU

At the beginning my wan face was seen at a few cock-tail parties, and people would come up and say, "I hear you're right down the toilet." I dreaded going out, and I dreaded going home to the tacky apartment I had rented, with disgusting leopard-skin sofas.

TINA BROWN, *VANITY FAIR*, THEN *NEW YORKER* EDITOR

I was rehabilitating this brownstone—when was it? Six years ago? Suddenly it came back to me. I'm an obsessive-compulsive! Back in the late twenties I worked in Palestine. And now I'm doing it all over again on the West Side—reclaiming ancient Jewish land.

MEYER LEVIN

It was Christmas Eve and I had a severe gall bladder attack. I had to take a cab to the [hospital], got out, and fell into the gutter. There I was, lying there, thinking, "Here I am a published writer, and I am dying like a dog." That's when I decided I would be rich and famous.

MARIO PUZO, AUTHOR, *THE GODFATHER*

The traditional pedestrian's right of way is, as Shakespeare says, "more honored in the breach than the observance". New Yorkers pay no attention whatsoever to WALK–DON'T WALK signs (it is just a part of that New York state of mind that asks: Why trust a sign? I have eyes!

THE NEW YORK TIMES GUIDE TO NEW YORK CITY

Visitors to New York will find that both exercise and excitement may be had at a minimum of expense through the simple practice of jay walking. With only a little experience, they may actually compete on even terms with the native New Yorker.

SIG SPAETH, *THE ADVANTAGES OF JAY WALKING*, 1926

Traffic signals in New York are just rough guidelines.

DAVID LETTERMAN

There are 12,000 licensed yellow taxis in New York City, and none appear to pick up fares in the rain.

FIONA DUNCAN AND LEONIE GLASS

Some of our worst congestion is caused by people in $30,000 autos driving to $100,000-a-year jobs who leave an expressway to save $2.

ROSS SANDLER, NYC TRANSPORTATION COMMISSIONER, 1987

I read big fat *Les Miserables* for weeks while I took the IRT subway for my Wednesday allergy shots. I needed to know Jean Valjean lived a more miserable life than I did.

E L. DOCTOROW, *LIVES OF THE POETS*

Well, Harry, are we wealthy or not?

CLARE BOOTH LUCE, TO HER HUSBAND, AFTER HE QUESTIONED HER ABOUT A $7,000 LINGERIE BILL

I used to see Mrs. Astor in her carriage, and she looked like a very silly woman to me. There were stories about her, that once she got on a bus and the driver passed the fare box to her. She said, "No thank you, I have my own charities."

MISS CORDELIA DEAL

An English visitor had been surprised to see none other than John Jacob Astor remove his chewing tobacco from his mouth and absent-mindedly trace a watery design with it on the windowpane.

STEPHEN BIRMINGHAM, *LIFE AT THE DAKOTA*

The rising generation of young elegants in America are particularly requested to observe that, in polished society, it is not quite *comme il faut* for gentlemen to blow their noses with their fingers, especially when in the street.

19TH CENTURY ETIQUETTE BOOK, CIRCA 1880

When a socialist harangued Andrew Carnegie about redistribution of wealth, Carnegie asked for his secretary for two numbers—the world's population and the value of all his assets. He divided the latter by the former, then said to his secretary, "Give this man 16 cents. That is his share of my net worth."

GEORGE WILL

I'll never do that again.

At the premiere of a documentary film about de Kooning, the film's narrator, Dustin Hoffman, mentioned an astronomical price brought at auction for a de Kooning painting. To the amazement of the audience, the artist's distinctive voice, marked by his flavorful Dutch accent, rose in the dark and still theater: "Jesus Christ!"

BENNETT SCHIFF

I've always loved decorating houses, my homes. And people say I have a knack for it. It's extremely demanding. I like to create the unexpected. If it's New York, I like to make a bedroom into a greenhouse. If it's London, I like to do something so exotic you don't notice the climate.

LEE RADZIWILL

———

I won the Italian of the Year twice in New York. I kept saying, "You don't understand. I can't accept this!"

JAMES CAAN ON *THE GODFATHER* CONNECTION

The summer of the [Son of Sam] killings was also one of the hottest ever on record in New York. Studio 54 had just opened, Plato's Retreat was in full swing, the punk scene was happening at CBGB's; and in addition, it was Reggie Jackson's first year with the Yankees.

SPIKE LEE

I met Billie Holiday when I was five. Miss Billie called me Mister Billy. The first blind man I ever saw was W. C. Handy. My father used to bring home jazz musicians at Passover. We had swinging seders.

BILLY CRYSTAL

My parents were on the conservative side. I was the last one to wear lipstick or a bra. But there was this little quirk of smoking grass. Not every night at dinner did we sit around and get stoned. On Passover, say, somebody would light a joint and we'd all sit and smoke it.

ELLEN BARKIN

I'd sit on his lap and watch. I was sitting there one night, when he put aside his work and taught me how to touch type. I was only six, but I took to it immediately and performed for him from time to time.

CHRIS BUCKLEY, ON A LESSON FROM HIS FATHER, WILLIAM F. BUCKLEY

It's essentially doing stand-up, but it's a little bit more interesting. Plus, the audience isn't drunk. I speak free to the Democrats and charge the Republicans. I've been hired by groups that say, "We're 95 percent Republican, so we want Al Franken, and we want him to shit all over the Republicans." And I basically do.

AL FRANKEN

There is a marvelous peace in not publishing. Publishing is a terrible invasion of my privacy. I like to write. I love to write. But I write just for myself and my own pleasure.

J. D. SALINGER

That [*New York Journal-American*] was a paper where, believe me, ya couldn't even believe the weather report.

JIMMY BRESLIN

Send dead roses. Dial 1–800–439–HATE and send someone special the first thing they really deserve!

AD IN *NEW YORK* MAGAZINE

Street Scenes

At three o'clock in the morning, when the rest of the city is silent and dark, you can come suddenly one a little area as vivacious as a country fair. In one bar, there is a little hunchback who struts in proudly, given free drinks, and treated as a sort of mascot.

CARSON MCCULLERS, "BROOKLYN IS MY NEIGHBORHOOD," *VOGUE*, 1941

New York had all the iridescence of the beginning of the world. The returning troops marched up Fifth Avenue and the girls were instinctively drawn east and north toward them—this was the greatest nation and there was gala in the air . . . whooping up our first after-the-war reunion.

F. SCOTT FITZGERALD, *THE CRACK UP*

Across the zinc water to the tall walls, the birchlike cluster of downtown buildings shimmered up the rosy morning like a sound of horns through a chocolatebrown haze. . . . Crammed on the narrow island the million windowed buildings will jut, glittering pyramid on pyramid.

JOHN DOS PASSOS, *MANHATTAN TRANSFER*

Harbors reveal a city's power, its lust for money and filth, but strangely through the haze what I distinguished first was the lone mellow promise of an island, tender retreat from straight lines. . .

Don DeLillo, *Great Jones Street*

The metaphor that many first-time visitors have employed is of the steam which rises from manholes at some street corners—part of an underground heating system for older buildings. They see this as a symbol of the city's latent energy.

Michael Leapman

I'm passing the joints on Fourteenth Street between Third and Fourth Avenues. I peeps under the swinging doors and keeps thinking that the swellest job in the world is the guy what bangs away on the piano. I wants to be him.

JIMMY DURANTE

The food was good café fodder and cheap and, at 2 A.M., helped to sober one up. Bill de Kooning usually stood at the bar.... Jackson Pollock, by then living in the Hamptons, might drop in while in New York. The tale is told that, one night, he tore the door off the men's room....

BENNETT SCHIFF, ON THE CEDAR STREET TAVERN IN GREENWICH VILLAGE

Once one gets off the main commercial streets, one finds that the 19th-century city is surprisingly intact and, in parts, is unusually handsome. . . .

L. J. DAVIS

Among those tangled irregular streets to the west of Washington Square, I caught occasionally, from the taxi, a glimpse, almost eighteenth-century, of a lamp-less, black-windowed street-end where the street-urchins, shrieking in the silence, were stacking up bonfires in the show.

EDMUND WILSON, *I THOUGHT OF DAISY*

She likes taxis. She travels in buses and subways only when she is trying to stop smoking. New York, the capsized city, half-capsized, anyway, with the inhabitants hanging on, most of them still able to laugh as they cling to their island that is their life's predicament.

MAEVE BRENNAN, *THE LONG-WINDED LADY: NOTES FROM THE NEW YORKER*

Evening is coming fast, and the great city is blazing there in your vision in its terrific frontal sweep and curtain of star-flung towers, now sown with the diamond pollen of a million lights, and the sun has set behind them, and the red light of fading day is painted upon the river.

THOMAS WOLFE

Ownerless pigs with battle-scarred ears amble about—and there are plenty of them here.

HENRYK SIENKIEWICZ, NOBEL PRIZE–WINNING NOVELIST, WHILE VISITING THE CITY IN 1876

New York is the concentrate of art and commerce and sport and religion and entertainment and finance, brining to a singe compact area the gladiator, the evangelist, the promoter, the actor, the trader and the merchant.

E. B. WHITE, *HERE IS NEW YORK*

The sun was low over the brownstones on the other side of the yard, and an ailanthus stood silhouetted against its golden rim, its budding branches forming a lace curtain through which a wind moved softly.

CHAIM POTOK, *THE CHOSEN*

High on the roof of one of the skyscrapers was a tin brass goat looking . . . out across silver snakes of winding rivers

CARL SANDBURG, *ROOTABAGA STORIES*

The city stretches from dollhouse rows at the base of the park through a broad blurred bell of flowerpot red patched with tar roofs and twinkling cars.

JOHN UPDIKE, *RABBIT, RUN*

———

Follow that couple carrying a bag of ice.

A COMMON WAY, IN SOHO, TO FIND AND CRASH A PARTY

The street where I now live has a quietness and sense of permanence that seem to belong to the nineteenth century. The street is very short. At one end, there are comfortable old houses, with gracious facades and pleasant back-yards in the rear.

CARSON MCCULLERS, "BROOKLYN IS MY NEIGHBORHOOD," *VOGUE*, 1941

I have the illusion of having put down roots here. I have spoken in most of the synagogues. They know me in some of the stores. Even the pigeons know me; the moment I come out with a bag of feed, they begin to fly toward me from blocks away.

ISAAC BASHEVIS SINGER, *A FRIEND OF KAFKA AND OTHER STORIES*

New York lay stretched in midsummer languor under her trees in her thinnest dress, idly and beautifully to the eyes of her lover.

E. B. WHITE, *POEMS AND SKETCHES OF E. B. WHITE*

It was one of those rainy late afternoons when the toy department of Woolworth's on Fifth Avenue is full of women who appear to have been taken in adultery and who are now shopping for a present to carry home to their youngest child.

JOHN CHEEVER

Mrs. O'Grady and the colonel's lady [are] close if uncommunicative neighbors. Here drying winter flannels are within fishpole reach of a Wall Street tycoon's windows, and the society woman in her boudoir may be separated only by a wall from the family on relief in a cold-water flat.

Lou Gody

———

At eighteen dollars a month, [our new apartment] was equipped with all sorts of conveniences that we Europeans were quite unused to: electric lights, gas cooking-range, bath, telephone, automatic service-elevator, and even a chute for the garbage. These things completely won the boys over to New York.

Leon Trotsky, *My Life*, 1930

The steaming clothes strung across the tenement kitchens; bathing the newest baby; the apartments without air, without light—there was never any ugliness or sordidness in all this for me.

FANNY BRICE

A tenement canyon hung with fire-escapes, bed-clothing, and faces. Always these faces at the tenement windows. The street never failed them. It was an immense excitement. It never slept. It roared like a sea. It exploded like fireworks.

MICHAEL GOLD, *JEWS WITHOUT MONEY*

When my parents moved to a more respectable and duller part of the city, it held no interest whatever for me. I hired a room in Hester Street in a wooden, ramshackle building that seemed to date back at least a hundred years and, from my window overlooking the market, made drawings daily.

JACOB EPSTEIN, *LET THERE BE SCULPTURE*

Any wall, any stoop, any curving metal edge on a billboard sign made a place against which to knock a ball; any bottom rung of a fire escape ladder a goal in basketball; any sewer cover a base; any crack in the pavement a "net" for the tense sharp tennis that we played . . .

ALFRED KAZIN, *A WALKER IN THE CITY*

The more gregarious arrange villages of their sections of the city, cultivating laconic chumminess in a local saloon or restaurant. The corner tailor freely offers his troubled autobiography after the second visit and the woman in the fish store is eager to teach Genoese tricks of fish cookery.

KATE SIMON

Mass is said in 23 different languages in this city.

ED KOCH, MAYOR, 1978–1989

A map of the city, colored to designate nationalities, would show more stripes than on the skin of a zebra, and more colors than a rainbow.

JACOB RIIS, *HOW THE OTHER HALF LIVES*

It is often said that New York is a city for only the very rich and the very poor. It is less often said that New York is also, at least for those of us who came there from somewhere else, a city for only the very young.

JOAN DIDION

Give me your tired, your poor, your huddled masses yearning to breathe free.

EMMA LAZARUS

———•••••———

The J train would with a certain wheezing ease through Queens and into Brooklyn. Birds could be heard, through the rumble, and graveyards and unopened schools flashed by outside the windows.

JOE SEXTON

Ride the New York subways one day. You could fall in love or get snake bitten or see a baby born. Hear a conductor do Elvis routines between stops. Buy a cabbage or a condom. . . . Every car on the local trains that leave the station will be filled to its "crush load" capacity of 180—and then, the records show, another 3.42 will pry themselves in.

JIM DWYER

Not everybody on the subway is demented. On the trains that call at Wall Street you will see businessmen and women, their clothes crumpled in the crush and heat, trying bravely to read the *Wall Street Journal* by folding it neatly in quarters.

MICHAEL LEAPMAN

Greater drama resides in the endless flow of activity that crowds the cars and platforms. Beggars, singers, banjo-players, and candy-butchers vie for a few pennies, howl bargains, or stumble silently past the apathetic passengers. Occasionally, a particularly bright singing troupe or an unusually pathetic cripple will meet with warm response.

LOU GODY

The city is itself a huge market. You can't go more than a few steps without finding a store of some sort. We are all potential entrepreneurs, looking to make a deal in this country of commerce.

JEROME CHARYN, *METROPOLIS*

Not to have seen those hucksters and their carts, and their merchandise, and their extraordinary zest for bargaining is to have missed a sight that once seen declines to be forgotten.

HARPER'S WEEKLY

Every detail matters. It is important to perceive that hardware stores are often painted orange out front, and that the color of newspaper kiosks and shoe shine stands is green.

NATHAN SILVER

"I really want those Gucci shoes," the good-looking young man told two friends as they walked across Prince Street. But one of them, a woman, was distracted. Pulling out her Nikon, she clicked away at a line of clean white laundry flapping from a line between two nearby brick tenements.

ANEMONA HARTOCOLLIS

On the east side, people buy their groceries a pinch at a time; three cents' worth of sugar, five cents' worth of butter, everything in penny fractions.

MICHAEL GOLD, *JEWS WITHOUT MONEY*

————•••••————

Small, inexpensive restaurants are the home fires of New York City.

MAEVE BRENNAN, *THE LONG-WINDED LADY: NOTES FROM THE NEW YORKER*

Men in the uniform of Wall Street retirement: black Chesterfield coat, rimless glasses and the *Times* folded to the obituary page.

JIMMY BRESLIN

If he chooses, his neighbors [may] remain hands only—the hand that holds an elevator on an upper floor, a hand that draws in a newspaper from an adjoining door mat, a hand that puts out a garbage pail or accepts a parcel.

KATE SIMON

I can see myself as a very old man in a terrific wheel chair. Only, I won't be photographing the tree outside my window, the way Steichen did. I'll be photographing other old people.

RICHARD AVEDON

These skyscrapers, who belong to a brotherhood of giants, help each other to rise, to prop each other up, to soar until all sense of perspective disappears. You try to count the stories one by one, then your weary gaze starts to climb in tens.

PAUL MORAND, *NEW YORK*

Every man seems to feel that he has got the duties for two lifetimes to accomplish in one, and so he rushes, rushes, rushes, and never has time to be companionable—never has any time at his disposal to fool away on matters which do not involve dollars and duty and business.

MARK TWAIN

He used to stage a ritual called 'Chasing Pigeons'. . . . [He would] charge madly into a flock of complacent pigeons, shouting and waving his arms. The pigeons would take to the air, but always come wheeling back, for no pigeon can resist his curiosity about an erratic human being.

ROGER BUTTERFIELD, ON THE STRANGE BEHAVIOR OF ACTOR ZERO MOSTEL

He blinked . . . and suddenly, he could see. He was crouching in the middle of a large meadow fringed with trees. Beyond the trees, wreathed in fog and mist, dozens of giant buildings were thrusting toward a leaden sky. There was a sign at the top of one of them: Essex House.

GEORGE CHESBRO, *BONE*

. . . set off with George Anthon and Johnny to explore the Central Park, which will be a feature of the city within five years and a lovely place in A.D. 1900, when its trees will have acquired dignity and appreciable diameters.

GEORGE TEMPLETON STRONG, *THE DIARY OF GEORGE TEMPLETON STRONG*

It has felt like 5:30 P.M. in the lobby of the Algonquin Hotel for nearly 90 years now . . . chronic, romantic twilight.

STEPHEN DRUCKER

———•••———

The night John died, there were so many people outside the Dakota. They were singing and playing John's songs. . . . Hearing his songs in the street was very difficult for me. I was sitting alone in our bedroom, which was on the 72nd Street side, and John was singing all night.

YOKO ONO

What Do New Yorkers Talk About When They Talk About Themselves?

My dream was to have a Library of Congress cata-
logue number, that's all.

FRANK MCCOURT, ON THE PUBLICATION OF *ANGELA'S ASHES*, HIS
FIRST BOOK

I don't mind being called Meathead.

ROB REINER, ON HIS LIFE AS ARCHIE BUNKER'S SON-IN-LAW

I'm sick to death of being a one-dimensional charac-
ter. I'm just a guy in a tight suit and a snap-brim hat.
I have no function except to carry the plot and get
killed in the end to prove that virtue is triumphant.

HUMPHREY BOGART

I have to be a little bit in love with my models. . . .

RICHARD AVEDON

When I go on the talk shows, I project what I am—
an intelligent and well-educated girl from Brooklyn.

BEVERLY SILLS

I knew I had talent and I was afraid that if I learned
to type I would become a secretary.

BARBRA STREISAND

No one seemed to care what I was doing so long as the record showed I had finished a full day's work. Therefore after lunchtime I kept my head bent low while I was writing short stories at my desk.

BERNARD MALAMUD, ON HIS CAREER STRATEGY AS A CLERK AT THE CENSUS BUREAU

I quit my job just to quit. I didn't quit my job to write fiction. I just didn't want to work anymore.

DON DELILLO

I think I've made a difference in my phase of the broadcast industry, but I don't think I've impacted on the world in the manner of Franklin Roosevelt.

HOWARD COSELL

Gore Vidal isn't what I set out to be. Early on I wanted to be Franklin Roosevelt.

GORE VIDAL

Not since *David Copperfield* have I read such a stirring and inspiring life story.

GROUCHO MARX, "REVIEWING" HIS OWN AUTOBIOGRAPHY

———

Once a song-and-dance man, always a song-and-dance man. Those few words tell as much about me professionally as there is to tell.

JIMMY CAGNEY

I always wanted to be some kind of writer or newspaper reporter. But after college—I did other things.

JACQUELINE KENNEDY ONASSIS

That was always my experience—a poor boy in a rich town; a poor boy in a rich boy's school; a poor boy in a rich man's club at Princeton...I have never been able to forgive the rich for being rich, and it has colored my entire life and works.

F. SCOTT FITZGERALD, IN A LETTER TO HIS AGENT'S WIFE

My father was the editor of an agricultural magazine called the *Southern Planter*. He didn't think of himself as a writer. He was a scientist, an agronomist, but I thought of him as a writer because I'd seen him working at his desk. . . . I just assumed that I was going to do that.

TOM WOLFE

So I started writing poetry when I was six. . . . when I was fifteen I wrote seven hundred pages of an incredibly bad novel—it's a very funny book I still like a lot.

EDWARD ALBEE

I assumed when writing it [Howl] that it was something that *could* not be published because I wouldn't want my daddy to see what was in there. About my sex life . . .

ALLEN GINSBERG

Very often I'll feel a certain shame for what I've done with a novel. I won't say it's the novel that's bad; I'll say it's I who was bad. Almost as if the novel did not really belong to me, as if it was something raised by me like a child.

NORMAN MAILER

When I'm finished with a piece, I'm embarrassed to look at it again, as I though I were afraid I hadn't wiped its nose clean.

J. D. SALINGER, IN A LETTER TO A FRIEND

———•••———

I'm a simple guy. For a comedian, I'm surprisingly normal. I have never been to a psychiatrist and I've only been married once.

JACK BENNY

When I'm close to finishing a book, nothing is more important to me. I might stop to save a life, but nothing less.

JOSEPH HELLER

If I'm going to be remembered as a novelist, I'd better produce a few more books.

RALPH ELLISON

When the lyrics are right, it's easier for me to write a tune than to bend over and tie my shoelaces.

RICHARD RODGERS

———

Of all my parents' friends, the only one happy going to work was a member of 120 Truck. I was only 16 then, but that is when I decided I wanted to be a fireman.

PETER J. GANCI JR., CHIEF OF DEPARTMENT, FDNY

I was about thirty-eight at the time, and thought I ought to get into abstractions, whatever they are. This attitude bewildered the instructors at several Paris art schools. . . . My best efforts were some modernistic things that looked like very lousy Matisses.

NORMAN ROCKWELL

I'd like to make a great film. I haven't made one yet. You don't start out to make a great film, you start out to make the idea you have at the time. But . . . maybe I'll get lucky and one or two will turn out to be terrific films.

WOODY ALLEN

I was brought up to be the . . . fat, happy child who would marry someone in the Racquet Club and drive around in a station wagon to pick up the twelve children and bring them home to the rose-covered cottage. Now I'm just the opposite, and I'm glad.

LEE RADZIWILL

I wanted a perfect ending. Now I've learned, the hard way, that some poems don't rhyme, and some stories don't have a clear beginning, middle, and end. Life is about not knowing, having to change, taking the moment and making the best of it.

GILDA RADNER

That whole show was completely beyond me. I never understood what was going on. They'd tell me to go over there and trip, so I'd go over there and trip.

BOB KEESHAN, AKA CAPTAIN KANGAROO, ON HIS EARLY WORK ON *THE HOWDY DOODY SHOW* AS CLARABELL THE CLOWN

———

It's my dream to be a member of the Rat Pack. I never thought about being a sitcom star. I thought about being Sammy Davis Jr.

TONY DANZA

I knew I was going to be a comedian at a very young age. I remember one time I made a friend laugh so hard he sprayed a mouthful of cookies and milk all over me, and I liked it.

JERRY SEINFELD

In kindergarten I flunked sandpile.

JOEY BISHOP

Carmela can cook, but God knows I can't.

EDIE FALCO, AKA CARMELA SOPRANO

———

I couldn't tell a joke if you put a gun to my head.

NEIL SIMON

I'm very proud of my Irish side also . . . I went there when I broke up with my girlfriend . . . [but] all you do is drink Guinness and cry and look at the ocean and want to kill yourself.

BEN STILLER

I never heard Archie's kind of talk in my own family. Mine was a family of teachers. . . . My father was a lawyer and was in partnership with two Jews. . . . There were two black families in our circle of friends. My father disliked talk like Archie's—he called it the hallmark of ignorance.

CARROLL O'CONNOR

If you live in New York, even if you're Catholic, you're Jewish.

LENNY BRUCE

I have no hobbies, no recreations. I hate sports. I also hate gardening and walking. I don't go to movies or the theatre or watch television. What I do like is lying down. My best thinking is done going into or coming out of naps.

JOSEPH HELLER

My first recorded success was at five years of age when I drew a cow with all her equipment. At eight I drew palm trees which I remember as being very fine. Fortunately, none has survived.

MARGARET AYER

The family had gone for a ride in the subway and when we came home I drew a picture of the conductor. The shape of his cap fascinated me. Anyway, my mother said, Sydney is an artist, and I've been trying to live up to her words ever since.

SYDNEY HOFF

We were smothered with opportunity—piano lessons, skating lessons, summer camps, art school. For a long time I wanted to be a painter. But there were so many painters in the family, and poetry was something nobody else did.

ERICA JONG

———

I touched it. It made pretty sounds. Right away I screamed, "Ma, give me lessons."

LEONARD BERNSTEIN, ON THE MOMENT HE FIRST TOOK INTEREST IN MUSIC

When I was a child, until the age of thirteen, I wanted passionately to be a chemist.

SUSAN SONTAG

He said it was because I loved horses, but I think he had this dream that I'd lose my accent.

PENNY MARSHALL, ON WHY HER FATHER SENT HER TO COLLEGE AT THE UNIVERSITY OF NEW MEXICO

I have an overly protective mother, and I never went out of my neighborhood until I became legal age. And then I just went over to the West Side, planted my foot down so I could say that I had been there, and ran right back home.

CHRIS ELLIOTT

One weird experience with matrimony made me respect the institution. I knew that I had broken a promise, a bargain, a contract. If I were to get into the habit of doing that, my word would not be worth the breath that spoke it in any other agreement.

MAE WEST, *GOODNESS HAD NOTHING TO DO WITH IT*

Women, horses, cars, clothes. I did it all. And do you know what that's called? It's called "living."

CAB CALLOWAY

I divide women into two categories. The female and the broad. Me? I'm a broad.

BETTE DAVIS

Every morning it takes me hours to get ready. The first time I saw myself naked in a school locker room, I was like, 'Wow.' After that, everything had to be trimmed, oiled and together.

CUBA GOODING JR.

I can't wait until tomorrow . . . because I get better looking every day.

JOE NAMATH

There's a million good-looking guys, but I'm a novelty.

JIMMY DURANTE

Well, I get on the bus; I put on my makeup; I study my notes; I read the paper. It's really—I'm really taking the bus because I'm cheap. . . .

HELEN GURLEY BROWN, *MANHATTAN PASSIONS*

People are afraid to hug me because they know I'm not a huggy guy.

RAY ROMANO

—•••◦—

I wound up putting a big sign on the front lawn listing all the people I didn't like. The list included the whole block, and I moved away amidst cheers and lawsuits.

JIMMY BRESLIN

If you pet me, I'll purr. But if you hit me, I might scratch.

LEONA HELMSLEY

I think I'm still an Impressionist.

EDWARD HOPPER

New York City Wisdom

Everybody credits me as saying that kissing Marilyn was like kissing Hitler. I never said that. I did more than kiss her . . . But we knew it was never going to work out between us, you know, rubbing and kissing doesn't always mean you're going to fall madly in love.

TONY CURTIS

Hollywood's a place where they'll pay you a thousand dollars for a kiss, and fifty cents for your soul. I know, because I turned down the first offer often enough and held out for the fifty cents.

MARILYN MONROE, *MARILYN MONROE IN HER OWN WORDS*

It's hard to convince a girl's parents that a revolutionary fugitive with a vasectomy is a good deal.

ABBIE HOFFMAN

Elephants are no harder to teach than ballerinas.

GEORGE BALANCHINE, ON HIS WORK DIRECTING RINGLING
BROTHERS' ELEPHANTS IN A BALLET

If you want to live a long time you have to smoke
cigars, drink martinis and dance close.

GEORGE BURNS

You got to be careful if you don't know where you're going, because you might not get there.

YOGI BERRA

———•••••———

To get as old as I am [91] one must drink a glass of whiskey every morning, smoke a long cigar and chase beautiful girls.

ARTHUR RUBINSTEIN

I've never had a hangover. I think it's because I don't smoke.

BERNARD "TOOTS" SHOR

———

Some of us are becoming the men we wanted to marry.

GLORIA STEINEM

If people would just take my advice, everything would go well.

WILLIAM F. BUCKLEY JR.

———•◦•———

I have been poor and I have been rich. Rich is better.

SOPHIE TUCKER

Money isn't everything as long as you have enough.

MALCOLM FORBES

———

If I knew I'd live this long, I would have taken better care of myself.

MICKEY MANTLE

One of the ways I save energy is by asking my servants not to turn on the self-cleaning oven until after seven in the evening.

BETSY BLOOMINGDALE

Nothing that costs only a dollar is worth having.

ELIZABETH ARDEN

If God called my office looking for advertising, I'd check out his references. You can never be too sure in this business.

Jerry Della Femina

It's OK to make money. It's a good thing. You go to heaven if you do it.

Ivan Boesky

I cannot justify approving monies to find out whether or not there is some microbe on Mars, when in fact I know there are rats in Harlem apartments.

ED KOCH, WHILE SERVING AS A MEMBER OF THE U.S. HOUSE OF REPRESENTATIVES

An author really hasn't made it until he no longer shows his books to his friends.

DOROTHY PARKER

Outlining a book is not writing. Researching is not writing. Talking to people . . . none of that is writing. Writing is writing.

E L. DOCTOROW

My whole theory of writing, I can sum up in one sentence. An author ought to write for the youth of his own generation, the critics of the next, and the schoolmasters of ever afterward.

F. SCOTT FITZGERALD

All I know about getting out a magazine is to print what you think is good (or as near to your standard as you can get) and let nature take its course: if enough readers think as you do, you're a success, if not you're a failure.

HAROLD ROSS, FOUNDER AND EDITOR OF *THE NEW YORKER*

I write on the right and I keep notes on the left, ideas that come, and then I pick them up later on. Then I go and sit at the keyboard and type it in and refine. So the pen for me is mightier than the word processor.

FRANK MCCOURT

The idea is to get the pencil moving quickly. I go over
and over a page. Either it bleeds and shows its begin-
nings to be human, or the form emits shadows of
itself and I'm off. I have a terrible will that way.

BERNARD MALAMUD

Just as Faulkner came from the South, I came from
Jewish Orthodox. And writers who write seriously,
write about what they know best.

CHAIM POTOK

I don't think any pregnant woman should read it, but the obstetrician did read it and loved it.

IRA LEVIN, AUTHOR OF *ROSEMARY'S BABY*, ON WHY HE WOULDN'T
LET HIS OWN WIFE READ THE BOOK

A writer in New York is a little bit like a tree falling in a forest. You're never sure if somebody's going to hear you.

LUCINDA FRANKS

A rising tide raises all ships.

ANONYMOUS WALL STREET ADAGE

———•••———

The worst part of having success is to try to find someone who is happy for you.

BETTE MIDLER

There may be said to be two classes of people in the world: those who constantly divide the people of the world into two classes and those who do not.

ROBERT BENCHLEY

———

I know that it is no longer the fashion to emphasize subject in fiction, but the more I read, the more I think it matters.

LOUIS AUCHINCLOSS

If you stay with newspaper work, you hit a point of no return, your talent levels out and diminishes, and . . . you retire without even knowing it.

DAVID HALBERSTAM

———•••———

You start with the philosophy that theater is important to people's lives. If you don't believe this, then you might as well give up.

JOE PAPP

I don't want it. Please don't impose on me something I don't want. . . . I know I should behave with more class, but there appears to be only one way to say no, and that's no.

THOMAS PYNCHON, DECLINING AN AWARD

School is bad for you if you have any talent. You should be cultivating that talent in your own particular way.

MAURICE SENDAK

When I was a little boy, they called me a liar, but now that I am grown up, they call me a writer.

Isaac Bashevis Singer

————

That is one last thing to remember: *writers are always selling somebody out.*

Joan Didion

Hell hath no fury like a hustler with a literary agent.

FRANK SINATRA, ON THE PUBLICATION OF JUDITH EXNER'S TELL-ALL
EXPOSE

In the theater only one man can count on steady work—night watchman.

TALLULAH BANKHEAD

I consider it immoral to go to the movies in the day-time.

PAULINE KAEL, *NEW YORKER* MAGAZINE MOVIE CRITIC

———

There is no such thing as a good painting about nothing.

MARK ROTHKO

Art is what you can get away with.

ANDY WARHOL

————— ❖ —————

Everybody can act, because everybody lies.

GEORGE ABBOTT

Televiso ergo sum—I am televised, therefore I am.

RUSSELL BAKER

No New Yorker should take Rupert Murdoch's *New York Post* seriously any longer. It makes *Hustler* magazine look like the Harvard (Law) Review.

ABE BEAME, MAYOR, 1974–1977

The singin's easy. Memorizing the words is hard.

ROCKY GRAZIANO, ON HIS NYC NIGHTCLUB DEBUT

If I had to give young writers advice, I would say, don't listen to writers talking about writing or about themselves.

LILLIAN HELLMAN

A good many young writers make the mistake of enclosing a stamped, self-addressed envelope, big enough for the manuscript to come back in. This is too much of a temptation to the editor.

RING LARDNER, *HOW TO WRITE SHORT STORIES*, 1954

—•••—

Red keeps you awake, don't you think?

MARY HIGGINS CLARK, ON HER CHOICE OF COLOR FOR THE WALLS IN HER OFFICE

A screenplay is a piece of carpentry, and except in the case of Ingmar Bergman, it's not an art, it's a craft. And you want to be as good as you can at your craft. . . .

WILLIAM GOLDMAN

Taking pictures is like tiptoeing into the kitchen late at night and stealing Oreo cookies.

DIANE ARBUS

I was drawing little Mickey Mouses for my children, working from bubble-gum wrappers. I thought I'd do one of the comics as is, large, just to see what it would look like.

ROY LICHTENSTEIN, ON THE BIRTH OF POP ART

———

I began life with the assumption that half the painters in the world were women.

ELAINE DE KOONING

I have friends who see themselves as the public sees them, and they are stone.

MIKE NICHOLS

———•·•·•———

I've come to realize that a big part of life is to smile when you turn in at night.

KAREEM ABDUL-JABBAR

Spoken Like a True
New Yorker

Truman could not tell you the truth about anything.
He was a psychopath, and the lies would get crazier
and crazier.

GORE VIDAL, ON TRUMAN CAPOTE

He is a sphinx without a secret.

TRUMAN CAPOTE, ON ANDY WARHOL

He decocts matters of the first philosophical magni-
tude from an examination of his own ordure, and I
am not talking about his books.

WILLIAM F. BUCKLEY, ON NORMAN MAILER

It is one of the sublime provincialities of New York
that its inhabitants lap up trivial gossip about essen-
tial nobodies they've never set eyes on, while contin-
uing to boast that they could live elsewhere folr
twenty years without so much as exchanging pleas-
antries with their neighbors across the hall.

LOUIS KRONENBERGER, *COMPANY MANNERS*, 1954

It's difficult to get terribly interested in food I digested 45 years ago.

DOROTHY PARKER, ON WHAT SHE AND HER FAMOUS WRITER FRIENDS ATE AT THEIR REGULAR HAUNT—THE ALGONQUIN ROUND TABLE AT THE ALGONQUIN HOTEL

A newspaper reported I spend $30,000 a year buying Paris clothes and that women hate me for it. I couldn't spend that much unless I wore sable underwear.

JACQUELINE KENNEDY ONASSIS

[New Yorkers are] people who get acquainted with their neighbors by meeting them in Miami.

MARJORIE STEELE

[Like] most native New Yorkers I was born out of town. . . .

HARRY HERSHFIELD, AKA MR. NEW YORK

I was aware that I didn't know anything about making films, but I believed I couldn't make them any worse than the majority of films I was seeing. Bad films gave me the courage to try making a movie.

STANLEY KUBRICK

My movies cost less than a director's salary on [an average film]. When you work as cheap as I do, the studio hands you the money and tells you to go off with your friends and have fun.

CHRIS GUEST

We wondered why all superheroes should be rich. Couldn't they be worried about money instead? The more we thought about these things, the more we enjoyed what we were doing.

STAN LEE, COMIC BOOK PUBLISHER

Success to me is having ten honeydew melons, and eating only the top half of each one.

BARBRA STREISAND

People seem to enjoy things more when they know a lot of other people have been left out of the pleasure.

RUSSELL BAKER

———•·•·•———

If Congress insists on making stupid mistakes and passing foolish tax laws, millionaires should not be condemned if they take advantage of them.

J. P. MORGAN

I may not look like a Senator, but I think I'm what a Senator should look like.

BELLA ABZUG

If you elect a matinee idol mayor, you're going to have a musical comedy administration.

ROBERT MOSES, ON NYC MAYOR JOHN V. LINDSAY

What do I care about the law? Hain't I got the power?

CORNELIUS VANDERBILT

———•◦•———

I'm not the type to get ulcers. I give them.

ED KOCH, MAYOR, 1978–1989

I could answer the question exactly the way you want, but if I did, I would hate myself in the morning.

RING LARDNER, TO THE HOUSE UN-AMERICAN ACTIVITIES COMMITTEE

—•••—

I can't cut my conscience to fit this year's fashions.

LILLIAN HELLMAN, TO THE HOUSE UN-AMERICAN ACTIVITIES COMMITTEE

People romanticize it. These were no giants. Think of who was writing in those days—Lardner, Fitzgerald, Faulkner, and Hemingway. Those were the real giants. The round table was just a lot of people telling jokes and telling each other how good they were.

DOROTHY PARKER, ON THE ALGONQUIN ROUND TABLE

My relatives say they are glad I'm rich, but that they simply cannot read me.

KURT VONNEGUT

The first night we had forty people out front and they didn't laugh at one of my jokes, but every time Gracie asked me a question, they fell out of their seats. So I made her the comic, and the act was a hit from that minute on. . . .

GEORGE BURNS

I hope to paint something that will ruin the appetite of every son of a bitch who ever eats in that room.

MARK ROTHKO, ON HIS COMMISSION FOR THE FOUR SEASONS RESTAURANT

What I wanted to do was to paint sunlight on the side
of a house."

EDWARD HOPPER

———•••••———

The outdoors is what you have to pass through to get
from your apartment to a taxicab.

FRAN LEBOWITZ

See that gold Cadillac down the street? That's the color I want those handrails. Gold. Cadillac gold. Not yellow like a daisy.

DONALD TRUMP, ON THE HANDRAILS IN TRUMP TOWER

—◆—

Donald has never had the net worth he claimed. What he did have was trophy properties, brass balls, and a big mouth.

A LAWYER FRIEND OF THE DONALD'S

We ought to change the sign on the Statue of Liberty to read, "This time around, send us your rich."

FELIX ROHATYN

Real equality is going to come not when a female Einstein is recognized as quickly as a male Einstein, but when a female schlemiel is promoted as quickly as a male schlemiel.

BELLA ABZUG, ACCORDING TO MARLO THOMAS

I'm going to tell people Jackie left it to me. After she said goodbye to the kids, she said, "Give this to Joan."

JOAN RIVERS, ON JACKIE ONASSIS'S COSTUME JEWELRY AND, IN PAR-
TICULAR, A GOLD AND BLACK-ENAMEL LIGHTER STAMPED WITH THE
INITIAL J.

We should have a secret meeting in the cellar of the St. James Theatre, raise $25 million, put on a million-dollar failure and split it up.

MEL BROOKS, ON THE SUCCESS OF HIS HIT MUSICAL THE PRODUCERS

I'll live to see the day, Sir, when you have to earn a living by going around Wall Street with a hand organ.

HENRY N. SMITH, FINANCIER

Maybe you will, Henry, maybe you will. And when I want a monkey, Henry, I'll send for you.

JASON GOULD, SMITH'S FORMER PARTNER, FINANCIER

Being an actor is like being a currency in the currency exchange. Today they are going, "Hey, you're the Deutsche mark. We think you're great. Wake up; it's not a dream." Then they turn around the next day and say, "Hey, we changed our minds. Somebody else is the Deutsche mark. You're the peso."

ALEC BALDWIN

Twenty-five bucks a week; hours from eight in the evening until unconscious.

JIMMY DURANTE, ON HIS JOB AT DIAMOND TONY'S SALOON ON CONEY ISLAND

Even though I know I look like a football player wearing a dress, in my mind's eye I'm beautiful.

HARVEY FIERSTEIN

In the '40s and '50s . . . men put on their dinner jackets. Women wore evening gowns. I wore evening gowns.

MILTON BERLE

I've been on a calendar, but never on time.

MARILYN MONROE

———•❖•———

It's not true that I had nothing on. I had the radio on.

MARILYN MONROE, ON POSING NUDE FOR A CALENDAR

We had like 600 kids in our graduating class, so I never met her. But I heard her. Every time I thought there was a fire drill, it was her.

RAY ROMANO, ON FRAN DRESCHER

⸺•❖•⸺

It's no fun being married to an electric light.

JOE DiMAGGIO, ON HIS MARRIAGE TO MARILYN MONROE

You know, I've actually had two children with the same woman. That's certainly a sign of maturity, don't you think?

JAMES CAAN

Even Superman can't make a commitment. Why give me a hard time?

JERRY SEINFELD

I have considered it. That's why I'm single.

> EVANGELINE BOOTH, GENERAL OF THE INTERNATIONAL SALVATION
> ARMY, WHEN A FRIEND SUGGESTED THAT SHE HAD REACHED AN AGE
> AT WHICH SHE SHOULD CONSIDER GETTING MARRIED

You know how to whistle, don't you, Steve? You just put your lips together and . . . blow.

> LAUREN BACALL, IN THE MOVIE *TO HAVE AND HAVE NOT*

It was love on the run with half the buttons undone.

MAE WEST, ON HER RELATIONSHIP WITH GEORGE RAFT

She told me to take off my pants. When I told her that I couldn't, because I didn't have any underwear on, she told me, "That's all right. If you had, I'd ask you to take it off too."

A BODYBUILDER AUDITIONING FOR MAE WEST

The city had beaten the pants off me. Whatever it required to get ahead, I didn't have. I didn't leave the city in disgust—I left it with the respect plain unadulterated fear gives.

JOHN STEINBECK, ON HIS FIRST STINT IN NEW YORK

Dancers are stripped enough onstage. You don't have to know more about them than they've given you already. I want to see people dance and I would like to guess what kind of people they are. I don't want to know the recipe for [their] pasta.

MIKHAIL BARYSHNIKOV

I dress for women—and I undress for men.

ANGIE DICKINSON

———

The world is an oyster, but you don't crack it open on a mattress.

ARTHUR MILLER, *DEATH OF A SALESMAN*

I think I made his back feel better.

MARILYN MONROE, REFERRING TO HER RELATIONSHIP WITH JFK

He was getting over a four-day drunk, and I was getting over a four-year marriage.

LILLIAN HELLMAN, ON HER FIRST MEETING WITH DASHIELL HAMMETT

A good saloonkeeper is the most important man in the community.

BERNARD "TOOTS" SHOR

My first qualification for this great office is my momumental personal ingratitude.

FIORELLO LA GUARDIA, TO JOB SEEKERS FOLLOWING HIS ELECTION

One of the brightest people I know is Shirley MacLaine, and Shirley is, of course, a firm believer in astrology. And in her defense I'll say this—that I have known Shirley MacLaine ever since she was a cocker spaniel and I . . .

STEVE ALLEN

She's gone to Bloomingdale's.

ANDY WARHOL, WHEN ASKED ABOUT HIS MOTHER'S DEATH

I bet you, Ziggie, a hundred bucks that he ain't here.

ATTRIBUTED TO THEATER PRODUCER CHARLES DILLINGHAM, WHIS-
PERED TO FLORENZ ZIEGFIELD AS THEY CARRIED HARRY HOUDINI'S
CASKET AWAY AS PALL-BEARERS

New York people will never go into a hole in the ground to ride . . . preposterous!

RUSSELL SAGE, ON THE NEWS IN 1900 NEWS THAT A RAILROAD WILL
BE BUILT BENEATH MANHATTAN

Meditation for most New Yorkers is thinking about their next apartment, the bigger one.

WILLIAM L. HAMILTON

In New York we simply assumed that we were the best—in baseball as well as intellect, in brashness and in subtlety, in everything—and it would have been unseemly to remark upon such an obvious fact.

MICHAEL HARRINGTON, *FRAGMENTS OF THE CENTURY*

Rolling Stone is not just about music, but also about the things and attitudes that music embraces. To describe it any further would be difficult without sounding like bullshit, and bullshit is like gathering moss.

JANN WENNER

It is true that I enjoyed my celebrity status in my previous position, but I can proved that when I left Washington I wore exactly the same size crown as when I arrived.

HENRY KISSINGER

Even in high school, I could write smoothly and well, long before I had anything to say.

LAWRENCE BLOCK

———

I won't quit until I get run over by a truck, a producer or a critic.

JACK LEMMON

When I go, I'll take New Year's Eve with me.

GUY LOMBARDO

———— ⚬·❉·⚬ ————

I agree with the Bogart Theory that all an actor owes
the public is a good performance.

LAUREN BACALL

If you don't like my identity, you won't like the magazine.

TINA BROWN, ON *VANITY FAIR*

—•••—

Neither has anyone else.

JOSEPH HELLER, ON COMPLAINTS THAT HE NEVER WROTE ANOTHER BOOK LIKE *CATCH 22*

A great many people have come up to me and asked me how I manage to get so much work done and still keep looking so dissipated. My answer is "Don't you wish you knew?"

ROBERT BENCHLEY, *HOW TO GET THINGS DONE*

I write out of outrage. My neighborhood, for example, pisses me off, with the drugs, crime, and homelessness. But I'm afraid of what happens the day I wake up and find I'm no longer angry about anything.

CALEB CARR

Freud's stupid. I didn't like Jung or Adler either. I go along with Samuel Goldwyn: he said anybody who has to see a psychiatrist ought to have to have his head examined.

MICKEY SPILLANE

I am not paranoid, and if you write that I am paranoid, I will personally sue *The New York Times*.

REX REED

If my film makes one more person miserable, I'll feel I've done my job.

WOODY ALLEN

———•••———

We're talking midlife crisis here. I miss my youth. I've got taxes to pay, I've got hemorrhoids, I don't have any real estate, I've got kids, and they got problems, and I'm nervous about the future.

ABBIE HOFFMAN

I'm spending about $600 a week talking to my analyst. I guess that's the price of success.

ROBERT DE NIRO

———•+•+•———

I occasionally have an anti-Roth reader in mind. I think, "How he is going to hate this!" That can be just the encouragement I need.

PHILIP ROTH

New York society has not taken to our literature. New York publishes it, criticizes it, and circulates it, but I doubt if New York society much reads it or cares for it, and New York is therefore by no means the literary centre that Boston once was.

WILLIAM DEAN HOWELLS, *LITERATURE AND LIFE*

Any real New Yorker is a you-name-it-we-have-it-snob . . . and his heart burns with sympathy for the millions of unfortunates who through misfortune, misguidedness, or pure stupidity live anywhere else in the world.

RUSSELL LYNES

You are an idiot. . . . You are in the presence of one of the great woman scholars of your time, and you behave like an ass, and you're gonna know about it when you're 50 years old. Eat my socks!

CAMILLE PAGLIA, DURING A 1992 VISIT TO PRINCETON UNIVERSITY

Tree is the number between two and four. *Jeintz* is the name of the New York professional football team. A *fit* is a bottle measuring seven ounces less than a quart. This exotic tongue has no relationship to any of the approved languages at the United Nations, and is only slight less difficult to master than Urdu.

FLETCHER KNEBEL

If I didn't get along with people, I just spent time by myself painting. And I didn't get along with people a lot.

JULIAN SCHNABEL

———•••———

If I ever had to practice cannibalism, I might manage if there were enough tarragon around.

JAMES BEARD

It's a place where everyone will stop watching a championship fight to look at an usher giving a drunk the bum's rush.

DAMON RUNYON, ON NEW YORK

Can we talk?

JOAN RIVERS

Bronx Cheers &
Other Sports News

Some kids want to join the circus . . . others want to be big-league baseball players. . . . When I came to the Yankees I got to do both.

GRAIG NETTLES, NEW YORK YANKEES

Does football keep you from growing up? Oh, my God, yes! One hundred per cent, yes! I've even heard guys who I thought had no minds at all admit that.

DAVID KNIGHT, NEW YORK JETS

There is no room in baseball for discrimination. It is our national pastime and a game for all.

LOU GEHRIG

———•••———

The highest prize in a world of men is the most beautiful woman available on your arm and living there in her heart loyal to you.

NORMAN MAILER, ON JOE DIMAGGIO'S MARRIAGE TO MARILYN MONROE

When we won the league championship, all the married guys on the club had to thank their wives for putting up with all the stress and strain all season. I had to thank all the single broads in New York.

JOE NAMATH

First date, July 30, 1966. I still have the actual ticket stubs. Mets game. I didn't even have a driver's licence. I had a double date with a guy named Eddie Cohen. And it was Casey Stengel's 75th birthday, and Eddie had four seats. So I said to [Janice], "You want to go?" she said, "Sure."

BILLY CRYSTAL, ON HIS FIRST DATE WITH JANICE GOLDFINGER, NOW HIS WIFE

Sure I played, did you think I was born at the age of 70 sitting in a dugout trying to manage guys like you?

CASEY STENGEL, WHEN ASKED BY MICKEY MANTLE IF HE HAD EVER PLAYED BALL

Till I was 13, I thought my name was "shut up."

JOE NAMATH

No one had ever been booed at a church's Communion breakfast before but they started howling at me as soon as they found out I was filling in for Joe DiMaggio.

PHIL RIZZUTO

It gets late early out there.

YOGI BERRA, ON THE COMING OF FALL AT YANKEE STADIUM

The team has come along slow but fast.

Casey Stengel

Your brain commands your body to "Run forward! Bend! Scoop up the ball! Peg it to the infield! Then your body says, "Who, me?"

Joe DiMaggio

Pitching is the art of instilling fear.

SANDY KOUFAX

———•◦•◦•———

That's why no boy from a rich family ever made the big leagues.

JOE DIMAGGIO

If he could cook, I'd marry him.

LEO DUROCHER, ON WILLIE MAYS

New Yorkers love it when you spill your guts out there. Spill your guts at Wimbledon and they make you stop and clean it up.

JIMMY CONNORS

You are the pits of the world! Vultures! Trash!

JOHN MCENROE, TO FANS, UMPIRES AND REPORTERS AT WIMBELDON

I wanted to kill him. I like him but I wanted to kill him.

ROCKY GRAZIANO, AFTER KNOCKING TONY ZALE OUT IN THE SIXTH

Everything you read about George Steinbrenner is true. That's the problem.

DAVE WINFIELD

———•••———

Winning means everything! You show me a good loser and I'll show you a loser.

GEORGE STEINBRENNER

The nice guys are all over there. In seventh place.

LEO DUROCHER, REFERRING TO THE LAST-PLACE NY GIANTS

———•••———

I was there when the flannel turned to double knit.

TOM SEAVER

Yells for the Mets were also yells for ourselves, a wry, half-understood recognition that there is more Met than Yankee in every one of us.

ROGER ANGELL, *ONCE MORE AROUND THE PARK*

Baseball people are generally allergic to new ideas . . . numbers on uniforms . . . spikes on a new pair of shoes. But they will [get together] eventually. They are bound to.

BRANCH RICKEY, GENERAL MANAGER, BROOKLYN DODGERS, ON THE INTEGRATION OF BASEBALL

There I was the black grandson of a slave, son of a black sharecropper, part of a historic occasion, a symbolic hero to my people . . . [but] I must tell you that it was Mr. Rickey's drama, and that I was only a principal actor.

JACKIE ROBINSON

———

I want a ballplayer with guts enough not to fight back. You will symbolize a crucial cause. One incident, just one incident, can set it back 20 years.

BRANCH RICKEY, TO JACKIE ROBINSON

Pro football is like nuclear warfare. There are no winners, only survivors.

FRANK GIFFORD

———•◦•———

There are three things you can do in a baseball game. You can win, or you can lose, or it can rain.

CASEY STENGEL

My greatest strength is that I have no weaknesses.

JOHN MCENROE

———•••———

All the time he's boxing he's thinking. All the time he was thinking, I was hitting him.

JACK DEMPSEY, ON HIS FIGHT WITH BENNY LEONARD

If you lose you're going to be fired, and if you win you only put off the day you're going to be fired.

LEO DUROCHER

It ain't over till it's over.

YOGI BERRA

The Day the World Trade Center Fell

They prayed that Timmy made it out alive. Then came the awful word.

U.S. NEWS & WORLD REPORT HEADLINE, OCTOBER 1, 2001

Nobody knew what had happened. Nothing. People were comforting one another. Someone said to me, "You know, you look kind of tired, buddy. Let me hold your jacket." And he did. Someone else asked to hold my briefcase. We made it all the way down. I don't know where those people are.

LOUIS LESCE

She said, "Oh, God, please save me," her friend said, clinging to a picture of her friend. "She was screaming that she was trapped and couldn't get out. She said, "I don't know what to do, I'm coughing, the heat is coming. I need water. I need water." And the phone dropped.

ANONYMOUS

I was in a lot of pain, and burned all over. Nobody had any idea what was going to happen to the buildings. So they were letting all of the people who were hurt go through. Everybody was helping each other.

MANU DHINGRA

His family is haunted by eerie signs of possible life. Rizzo's pager, which is with him, keeps receiving messages. So they page him and page him, hoping that rescuers will hear the signal from under the rubble.

LYNN JORDAL-MARTIN, FOX NEWS

Let those who say that we must understand the reasons for terrorism come with me to the thousands of funerals we are having in New York City and explain those insane, maniacal reasons to the children who will grow up without fathers and mothers, to the parents who have had their children ripped from them for no reason at all.

RUDOLPH W. GIULIANI

The last time anyone saw Ganci, the mayor said, he had just ordered the men in his command post to move north to safety. Ganci, himself, then turned back into the disaster area to check on more firefighters. "I am always amazed at how these men walk into fires, when the rest of us run from them," he said.

SALLY JENKINS, *THE WASHINGTON POST*

———•—•—•———

I weep and mourn with America. I wish I could comfort every single family whose lives have been affected.

GEORGE W. BUSH

Everybody called her "Grammy," but her name was Thelma Cuccinello, and she was 71.... "I was the last one to see her," [her daughter Cheryl] O'Brien said. "I got to kiss her and say 'I love you' and 'Have a nice trip.' "

CHRISTY OGLESBY, CNN

You never had to see her to know that she was in a room. You just knew her laugh. She always found a reason to laugh.

BRIAN HULL, ON HIS FRIEND, VALERIE SILVER ELLIS (*NEW YORK TIMES*)

What do I tell the pilot to do?

BARBARA OLSON, CNN COMMENTATOR, IN HER LAST WORDS TO
HER HUSBAND TED, THE U.S. SOLICITOR GENERAL

It really came home when I saw guys go in those buildings, and the number that didn't come out . . .

CECIL PULLIAM

I really believe that if they sent them to hell they would put it out. The World Trade Center collapse was worse than hell.

RUSSELL BEST, CREATOR OF A REALITY TV SHOW ABOUT FIREFIGHTERS CALLED *THE BRAVEST*

He said, "I want you to know I love you very much, and I'm calling you from the plane. We've been taken over."

ALICE HOGLAN, ON HER SON, MARK BINGHAM, KILLED ON UNITED AIRLINES FLIGHT 93

I'm on the plane that's been hijacked . . . there's three of us who are going to do something about it."

THOMAS BURNETT JR., TO HIS WIFE FROM UNITED AIRLINES FLIGHT 93

Let's roll.

TODD BEAMER, AS HE AND OTHER PASSENGERS ON UNITED AIRLINES FLIGHT 93 STRUCK BACK AGAINST THE TERRORISTS

They are the names of passengers who defied their murderers and prevented the murder of others of the ground. They are the names of men and women who wore the uniform of the United States and died at their posts. They are the names of rescuers whom death found running up the stairs to rescue others.

GEORGE W. BUSH

————

The children are devastated. They keep asking every night, "Where's Daddy? Well, Mommy, we watched *Cast Away*. He came back after four years, so maybe Daddy will come back."

ANNE WODENSHEK

Near one revolving door, some people handed a bleeding blond woman to Guadagnoli and a news photographer snapped a shot of him cradling her, an image soon seen around the world. "I told her, 'Don't worry.' I said, 'Just squeeze my hand if you feel pain,' and boy, did she squeeze hard."

PATRICIA HURTADO, *NEW YORK NEWSDAY*

"My wife wants to know how he died," said one man recently about his missing son. "Did he suffer? Was he crushed? Did he fall? Me, I just hope he didn't suffer."

JON KYL, U.S. SENATOR

He took his hat off to pray, and something came
down and hit him in the head.

BOB MCGRATH, RETIRED BATTALION CHIEF, ABOUT FDNY'S FATHER
MYCHAL JUDGE

A new shift of police officers pushes through the wall
of believers, everyone polite, and tourists press flow-
ers on the men and women in blue as they cross
under a street sign, left over from Yankee baseball
ticker-tape parades. It says, "Broadway, Canyon of
Heroes."

MARC FISHER, THE WASHINGTON POST

We were asked as children what we wanted to be when we were older we would answer, "A fireman, a policeman." Today as adults, we again answer, "We want to be like them."

RABBI JOSEPH POTASNIK, FDNY CHAPLAIN, AT THE PRAYER SERVICE AT YANKEE STADIUM

Rescuers would often arrive to eat and, exhausted, lay their heads on the table to sleep. When they awoke they'd use the bathroom to wash their faces and go back out.

KURT GENDEN, OF THE REGENT HOTEL ON WALL STREET

We decided to make this for you because peanut butter and jelly sticks together like you guys have stuck together to help America.

A LETTER FROM STUDENTS AT SYLVIA CIRCLE ELEMENTARY SCHOOL IN ROCK HILL, SOUTH CAROLINA

—•—

... a 13-year-old boy named Cameron, whose brother worked on the 104th floor of one of the towers. U.S. News & World Report reported that after the collapse of the building, Cameron called his brother's cell phone, which was still taking messages. "He just wanted to talk to him one last time," said his father.

JON KYL, U.S. SENATOR

I'm a loving guy. And I am also someone, however, who's got a job to do and I intend to do it. And this is a terrible moment.

GEORGE W. BUSH

"Have you seen . . . ?" begins each flyer photocopied and pasted on dozens of walls of hope around the city. Someone's father, someone's sister. Below each picture are the minutae of their existence—every mole, every piece of jewelery, every scar. Perhaps they are injured and unconscious in some hospital, or one of the John or Jane Does.

MICHELE MANDEL, *THE CALGARY SUN*

The evidence of terrorism's brutality and inhumanity, of its contempt for life and its contempt for peace, is lying beneath the rubble of the World Trade Center less than two miles from where we meet today. Look at that destruction, that massive, senseless, cruel loss of human life, and then I ask you to look in your own hearts and recognize that there is no room for neutrality on the issue of terrorism.

RUDOLPH W. GIULIANI, IN AN ADDRESS TO THE UN

Now we understand much more clearly, why people from all over the world want to come to New York and to America. It's called freedom.

RUDOLPH W. GIULIANI

Today, we come together to confess our need of God. Those perpetrators who took us on to tear us apart, it has worked the other way. It has backfired; it has brought us together.

BILLY GRAHAM, AT THE PRAYER SERVICE AT THE NATIONAL CATHEDRAL

Close to home, a desire to triumph over evil led Continental Airlines gate agent Susan Golden to reach out to travelers marooned at Hartsfield. She took 18 of them to her house, served them pizza and found them places to sleep. "There's too much goodness in the world to let darkness overcome us," she said.

THE ATLANTA CONSTITUTION

At a time like this, the only saving grace is our common humanity and decency.

JEAN CHRÉTIEN, CANADIAN PRIME MINISTER

After George Washington was inaugurated the first President of the United States, in New York City, he walked to St. Paul's, and he kneeled down to pray. The pew where he worshipped is still there. For the past 25 years, the chapel stood directly in the shadow of the World Trade Center Towers. When the Towers fell, more than a dozen modern buildings were destroyed and damaged. Yet somehow, amid all the destruction and devastation, St. Paul's Chapel still stands, without so much as a broken window.

RUDOLPH W. GIULIANI, AT THE CITYWIDE PRAYER SERVICE AT YANKEE STADIUM

If I know Andrew, he stopped to help somebody. . . . I don't want to think about what happened to him, but he's just not here.

ERICA ZUCKER, ABOUT HER HUSBAND, ANDREW

All it's done is made both children very strong and very determined in what they've set out to do. They're not going to let this setback stop them from the dreams they and their father had.

SARAH TAYLOR, ON HER HUSBAND, DONNIE, *THE NEW YORK TIMES*

Index